D1279574

Botkin:

THE PRACTICAL STRATEGIES SERIES
IN GIFTED EDUCATION

series editors
FRANCES A. KARNES & KRISTEN R. STEPHENS

Assessment in the Classroom: The Key to Good Instruction

Carolyn M. Callahan

PRUFROCK PRESS, INC.

Printed in the United States of America.

ISBN-13: 978-1-59363-191-8
ISBN-10: 1-59363-191-X

At the time of this book's publication, all facts and figures cited are the most current available. All telephone numbers, addresses, and Web site URLs are accurate and active. All publications, organizations, Web sites, and other resources exist as described in the book, and all have been verified. The authors and Prufrock Press, Inc., make no warranty or guarantee concerning the information and materials given out by organizations or content found at Web sites, and we are not responsible for any changes that occur after this book's publication. If you find an error, please contact Prufrock Press, Inc. We strongly recommend to parents, teachers, and other adults that you monitor children's use of the Internet.

Prufrock Press, Inc.
P.O. Box 8813
Waco, Texas 76714-8813
(800) 998-2208
Fax (800) 240-0333
http://www.prufrock.com

Contents

The Practical Strategies Series in Gifted Education offers teachers, counselors, administrators, parents, and other interested parties up–to–date instructional techniques and information on a variety of issues pertinent to the field of gifted education. Each guide addresses a focused topic and is written by scholars with authority on the issue. Several guides have been published. Among the titles are:

*   *Acceleration Strategies for Teaching Gifted Learners*
*   *Curriculum Compacting: An Easy Start to Differentiating for High-Potential Students*
*   *Enrichment Opportunities for Gifted Learners*
*   *Independent Study for Gifted Learners*
*   *Motivating Gifted Students*
*   *Questioning Strategies for Teaching the Gifted*
*   *Social & Emotional Teaching Strategies*
*   *Using Media & Technology With Gifted Learners*

For a current listing of available guides within the series, please contact Prufrock Press at (800) 998-2208 or visit http://www.prufrock.com.

The major goal of instruction is to maximize the learning of all students in the classroom. With that goal in mind, a teacher can clearly see his or her desired outcomes for the activity, lesson, or unit that is planned. However, appropriate selection of these end goals and success in achieving an environment in which all learners are fully engaged in the learning process depends on a clear awareness of the current academic status of all students in the classroom. It is, therefore, critical to take into account the current level of knowledge, understandings of concepts, beliefs, skills, and dispositions (e.g., willingness to engage in critical thinking) of students in the classroom, as well as their wide range of interests and preferred learning styles. In heterogeneous classrooms, differences in student knowledge, skills, and understandings are often striking. The range of differences within a group of gifted students at any grade level is likely to be vast, as well. Like any group of students, gifted students differ in the ways they prefer to process information, in the ways they approach learning, in what motivates them, and in the values they bring to the learning process.

The National Research Council (NRC; Bransford, Brown, & Cocking, 1999) documents "that learning is enhanced when teachers pay attention to the knowledge and beliefs that learners bring to a learning task, use this knowledge as a starting point for new instruction, and monitor students' changing conceptions as instruction proceeds" (p. 11). The NRC also affirms the importance of motivation in influencing the amount of time a student will commit to learning, and of setting an appropriate level of challenge in a task for such motivation to be sustained. When a task is too difficult students are frustrated and lose motivation, and when a task or learning activity is too easy students are bored and unmotivated.

The current understanding of the ways in which learning occurs suggests that new knowledge must be built on existing knowledge *and* that existing knowledge greatly influences how students process new knowledge (Cobb, 1994; Piaget, 1978; Vygotsky, 1978). As a consequence, the NRC concluded that "effectively designed learning environments must be assessment centered" (Bransford et al., 1999, p. 127); that for the greatest amount of student learning success, classroom instruction must include opportunities for feedback and revision, as well as summative, conclusive assessment; and that the content of summative assessment must reflect a close match between what is assessed and the instructional learning goals. Therefore, to provide the most effective classrooms for gifted students, we must look at the instructional process and identify ways to best infuse assessments so instruction is planned to maximize their learning.

The process of planning and implementing instruction must be looked at as a cyclical process rather than a linear one, with the results of one instructional cycle forming the basis for the next set of decision making. The first step in the instructional cycle is to examine the current status of the students in the classroom. While the present educational environment is characterized by strong accountability tied to student achievement of a particular set of state or local standards, it is quite possible that some students—most especially gifted learners—have already mastered some or all of the knowledge, understanding, or skills outlined in these goals. In other cases, gifted students may have demonstrated some level of achievement, but the standards provide for a very high ceiling of achievement, which can then be used to set advanced levels of expected outcomes in terms of the depth, complexity, and difficulty of the content, the sophistication of the skills learned, or the quality of products used to demonstrate learning. Students who have already mastered a given level of performance on an objective should not be spending their valuable learning time engaged in activities to achieve those same outcomes. The curricular objectives and instructional activities for these students should be accelerated or enriched.

Likewise, those with a particular level of skill, knowledge, or understanding should be challenged with more open-ended goals in order to reach new levels of accomplishment. For example, one of the standards in a language arts curriculum may be: *Students write for a variety of purposes and audiences, developing a style and voice.*[1] While the assessments and examples provided for the average student statewide will set a standard of acceptable achievement of this objective, it is easy to see that the same generic goal could be included in a creative writing course at the graduate level of study. Hence, the teacher of a gifted student needs to assess his or her current level of performance and strive to set higher standards or goals for the gifted student so that he or she ascends to the next level of performance.

Accurate assessment of the student's level of content knowledge, understanding, and skills is critical for setting the goals of instruction because the most effective learning will occur when the tasks presented to the learner are in the band identified by Vygotsky (1978) as the zone of proximal development. To create lessons that are within a student's zone of proximal development, teachers must determine where the student currently stands—assessing the difference between what a student can do independently and what the student can do with the guidance of an adult or more advanced peer. The planning process should incorporate tasks that are just beyond the point where the student can do the task without any assistance and should also incorporate learning activities that may require some guidance by an adult or peer in their execution, so that new learning will occur.[2] Ideally, such learning will lead to the student acquiring the knowledge, understanding, and

[1] Taken from the Language Arts Standards for 4th grade in the state of California.
[2] The discussion of appropriate teaching strategies is beyond the scope of this monograph but might include didactic instruction, interactive instruction, or collaborative learning and might include a wide range of strategies from cubing, to rafting, inquiry-based activities, experimentation, group investigations, learning contracts, varied questioning strategies, literature circles, etc.

skill ability to carry out a parallel task independently. In sum, accurately setting the level of cognitive functioning at the onset of an instructional cycle is necessary.

As noted earlier, it is critical to create a strategy for collecting data as an instructional unit evolves. While gifted learners often learn at a faster pace, there is still considerable variability among them. Therefore, developing strategies for monitoring learning as a unit progresses is important to ensure that the learning process is proceeding appropriately. Checking on the progress of learning also allows for acceleration of pace or the addition of increased levels of complexity. Such monitoring also provides guidance for adjustments if students have misunderstandings, need additional support, or have unexpected gaps in prerequisite skills or knowledge. Furthermore, teaching students to monitor or assess their own learning is critical in developing independent, self-directed learners.

Finally, the data collected on the outcomes of instruction become the basis of creating a new learning cycle, as it provides valuable information on the accomplishment of prior goals. Rather than taking a position that one must simply teach whatever comes next in the sequence of prescribed objectives and topics, using the assessments from prior units provides information ensuring prerequisite understanding is in place for subsequent units. Summative assessment also provides critical information for parents and students in helping them evaluate the degree to which goals and objectives are being accomplished.

Before embarking on a discussion of how to approach assessment of gifted learners in the classroom, two fundamental concepts must be reviewed. The first of these is *reliability*. The reliability of an instrument is the degree to which its scores measure a variable. In all assessment, the data must be as free of random error as possible. That is to say, the measure of a student characteristic should not vary greatly from day-to-day due to factors unrelated to the variable being measured (e.g., luck, unclear test items, mood, fatigue, boredom, unclear scoring guidelines). For example, if an instructional decision is based on a student's skill in locating credible primary source material, it must be certain that an estimate of proficiency is not based on a test where the student was just lucky that the items were about the one or two primary sources he or she happened to be familiar with, or that the student was a good guesser on that particular day. Similarly, if a task is based on the assessment of a student's interest in a given topic, it must be certain that responses provided on an assessment of interests are not influenced by something like a television program viewed the night before.

Even more important than reliability is the *validity* of a measure. It is crucial that assessments measure the underlying construct that is trying to be measured and not some other variable. For example, in assessing a student's knowledge of science concepts, a teacher must be certain that the understanding of science, and not reading ability, is being measured. Or if a teacher is assessing a student's interests, those interests should be measured, not the student's perception of something socially desirable or teacher pleasing.

If the measures selected or constructed to assess students are reliable and valid, then decisions made based on the data collected from such measures will contribute to better instructional planning and more accurate communication of the results of instruction. When correctly executed, such data-based decision making creates an effective instructional model.

Data-Based Decision Making: Assessing the Status of Students

There are four dimensions of particular interest in collecting data on gifted students for effective instructional planning: aptitude, achievement, interests, and learning style/performance preferences. Acting on data about a student along each of these dimensions offers the potential for enhanced learning. Aptitude and learning style tend to be relatively stable variables, while interests and achievement are more variable based on the particular discipline, the topic to be studied within that discipline, and a student's life experiences. The stability of a variable is important in consideration of how often and under what conditions a teacher might collect data and modify instruction accordingly.

Aptitude

The collection of aptitude data can ensure that a teacher has set appropriate levels of complexity and pacing for instruction. Sample aptitude measures might include the Scholastic Aptitude Test (SAT), the Cognitive Abilities Test (CogAT), individual and group intelligence tests such as the Wechsler

Scales, and the Differential Aptitude Tests (DAT). Such measures reflect the degree to which students have developed advanced skills in reasoning and thinking in either general areas or within specific cognitive domains (e.g, verbal ability, quantitative reasoning, spatial reasoning, etc.).

Aptitude data offers information on how rapidly a student learns, the degree to which the student can process information with understanding, and the general reasoning ability of the student. Such data is generally available from student records, and some indication of general aptitude can probably be gleaned from the test identification protocols used in the school district. Tests such as intelligence tests and general and specific aptitude tests yield general data that is relatively stable. Scores on these tests are considered very reliable for up to 2 years (after the primary school years, when the scores are not very reliable). General aptitude data will provide the approximate relative speed with which a learner might master new information and concepts. Specific aptitude data will provide information on expected learning ability in one discipline. However, this data is very general and gives only rudimentary guidance.

In some cases, aptitude has been assessed by teacher observations and ratings. Students may be rated by current or former teachers on their learning capabilities, and the instruments used may provide subjective information from other professionals on students' past learning behavior. For example, if the Scales for Rating the Behavioral Characteristics of Superior Students (SRBCSS) has been used, examination of the completed scales will give relative ratings of past behavior and potential in the areas of learning, creativity, motivation, leadership, art, communication, mathematics, science, and technology, among others (Renzulli et al., 2004). Particular items within this scale and from other teacher rating scales may provide some information on learning potential in general and in specific academic areas.

Achievement

Data collected during the identification process will likely include general achievement data from standardized achievement tests. Examples of commonly used achievement tests include the Iowa Tests of Basic Skills (ITBS) and the Stanford Achievement Series (Stanford 10). Scores from these tests, like the aptitude data, give a general indication of relative performance in the traditional subject matter areas at the time of the assessment. Achievement data of this type should be used to guide the teacher in identifying areas where there is an expectation that students have attained mastery or will likely be able to quickly attain proficiency at the grade levels specified in the general curriculum. The subscales of the comprehensive tests and the patterns of responses on an individual subtest are often provided in conjunction with specific sets of objectives measured by the items (e.g., measurement might be a category of items on a mathematics subscale). In addition, specific scales like the Test of Mathematical Abilities for Gifted Students (TOMAGS; Ryser & Johnsen, 1998) may have been used to screen for or identify specific talent areas and can provide information on mathematical concepts tied to the curriculum standards of the National Council of Teachers of Mathematics such as number sense and numeration, whole number operations, geometry, statistics, and probability.

Standardized achievement test scores are usually reported in percentile ranks or grade equivalent scores. Percentile ranks tell us where the student performed relative to those who were included in the norm or comparison group, as identified by the test publisher. For example, if a student earns a score in the 99th percentile in mathematics concepts, then 99% of the norm group scored at or below that student. A grade equivalent score is trickier to interpret and is, therefore, often misinterpreted. A grade equivalent score of 4.6 means that the student scored at the mean for students who were in the 6th month of 4th grade. A reading score of 8.8 does not mean the student is reading at the eighth grade level. Rather, it means the student earned the same score as the average student in the eighth month of eighth grade. Teacher rating scales, report cards, and permanent record data will also provide a general estimate of student achievement in specific disciplines.

Standardized achievement test data is a general gauge, but there are two drawbacks to using it for specific instructional decision making with gifted students. First, it provides only a very broad assessment of achievement in the discipline rather than data that is relative to what might be planned for the next instructional unit. Additionally, on-grade-level achievement testing of gifted students often fails to indicate the actual level of performance of the student because the ceilings on grade-level tests are often too low. That is, gifted students may be able to perform even more difficult and advanced tasks than those presented in grade-level assessments.

More importantly, data collected for identification purposes or recorded on report cards will not give specific information that can be used as a guide in determining what a student knows about the upcoming unit or module of study. To accurately assess the students' knowledge, understanding, and skills, it is necessary to either identify or select an assessment tool specifically designed to measure a particular area of study. One likely source of data in some subject areas are pretests often found in teacher's manuals. A final task or exam from a prior year's instruction may serve as a pretest with a new group, or a brief self-report survey can be developed for students to complete. For example, in a unit for grades 6–7 on colonization of the New World, the student might complete a quick pretest like the one found in Figure 1. Items on this pretest progress from very easy to more complex so the level at which the student is functioning can be estimated. Note that the latter questions become more open-ended, allowing for greater opportunity for the gifted students to show the extent of their knowledge and understanding.

Colonization of the New World

We are going to study the colonization of the New World. There were 13 original colonies and each of them was founded by a separate group of people and had a unique history up until the American Revolution. I want to see how much you already know about the colonies. This is not a test for a grade, but I want you to do your very best to answer these questions. If you do not know an answer, that is okay. We will be studying about the colonies so you will have a chance to learn.

How many of the original 13 colonies can you name? List all those you can think of in the space below.

On the map of the United States below, place a dot on the map locating the colonies you know and label each colony.

What were some of the reasons that the colonists left their homelands to come to the New World?

What are some similarities across all the colonies?

What are some of the differences between the colonies?

Choose one of the original 13 colonies. Name two people who lived in that colony and tell me as much about each of them as you can.
    1.

    2.

Figure 1. Pretest on colonization of the New World

If students have been using graphic organizers, an alternative assessment might entail giving the students a graphic organizer such as the one found in Figure 2. In the case of preparing for a unit on colonization, teachers may ask students to identify a colony they know the most about and complete the graphic organizer. If students complete one sheet accurately, provide additional sheets and have them choose a second colony. Having each student choose a colony that he or she knows very little about will also provide a sense of the student's breadth of knowledge on this topic. Students may even be asked to estimate their own level of understanding. See Figure 3 for an example of a student self-assessment for this unit.

In assessing achievement, it is also important to determine the degree to which the students have attained information processing skills, and if sophisticated results are to be produced, the degree to which students have mastered the skill of successful production.

Interests

Because interest is a motivation factor, it has a particularly important place in the preassessment process. An area of interest can be tied to general or specific topics in a unit. Generalizations about gifted students and their interests and motivations can lead to selection of general topics to motivate students, and to the creation of "hooks" that will initially engage students in a topic. General assessments of interest can be carried out at the beginning of the year and used for many decisions, but a teacher may elect to gather specific information when such assessment data does not prove helpful for designing specific lessons within a topic or offering alternatives in the creation of products to demonstrate learning. For example, the Interest-A-Lyzer (Renzulli, 1997) might be used early in the school year with elementary and middle school children to survey general interest areas. This instrument will provide information on student interests across the domains of performing

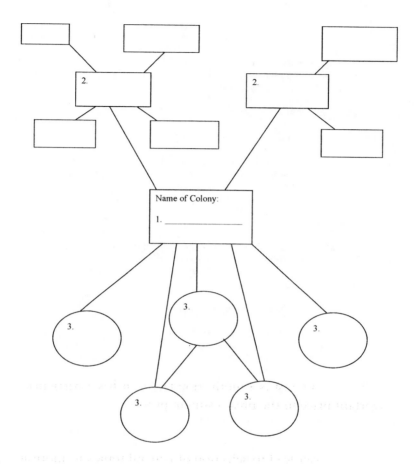

Use the graphic organizer to show what you already know about one of the original 13 colonies. Write the name of the colony that you are most familiar with in the space marked 1. Write the names of two people associated with the colony in the boxes labeled 2. Write down some actions or characteristics of the person you have named in the rectangles associated with 2. Write as many things that you know about the colony in the circles marked 3. You may add other circles or rectangles if you know more.

Figure 2. Using a graphic organizer as preassessment

Are You The Expert?

We are about to study the colonization of the New World. I want to know what you already have learned about the original 13 colonies. Think for a minute about what you have learned in the past on this topic and then answer each of the questions below. This is NOT a test and you will not be graded.

Circle the category that best describes you.

I can name the 13 colonies:

I know the names of all 13.	I can name 4–8 colonies.	I can name one of the colonies.	I don't know the names of any of the colonies.

I can tell about the history of all of the colonies:

I know so much I could write a story about each one.	I could tell you a few things about a few of the colonies.	I know a little bit about one of the colonies.	I don't know the history of the colonies.

I can describe the similarities among the colonies:

I can name several ways the colonies were alike.	I know at least two ways the colonies were alike.	I cannot think of any ways the colonies were alike.

I can describe the differences between the colonies:

I can name several ways the colonies were different.	I know at least two ways the colonies were different.	I cannot think of any ways the colonies were different.

I know about the people who settled the colonies:

I know so much I could write a story about them.	I could tell you a few things about a few of the people.	I know a little bit about the people.	I don't know the people who settled the colonies.

I can name some of the important historical people who lived in the colonies and tell about their lives.

I know so much I could write a story about one from each colony.	I could tell you a few things about a few of the historical figures.	I know a little bit about one of the historical figures.	I don't know the historical figures.

Figure 3. Student self-assessment

arts, creative writing and journalism, mathematics, business/management, athletics, history, science, technology, and the like. Most published interest inventories relate to vocational interests and are designed for high school students (e.g., the Strong-Campbell Interest Inventory or the Kuder General Interest Survey), but the results, which give relative interest in areas such as agriculture, military activities, mechanical activities, science, mathematics, music/dramatics, art, athletics, and law and politics, can be used to get a general sense of student interest.

However effective the design of a specific instructional unit, it will be more effective if student interests as they relate to that unit are assessed. Consider the student interest survey in Figure 4. This interest inventory provides specific information that guides the choice of readings and activities, and offers a sense of student readiness. In constructing such an inventory, the teacher should provide an opportunity for students to express already developed interests and potential interests. Asking students about what they like to think about and do in their spare time may serve as a basis for an inventory. For example, giving students a list of noted persons during the Roaring Twenties with brief descriptions about what they contributed, and then asking students to rank them according to their own interest will provide a brief outline of individual preferences. Teachers can also ask if students would prefer to study the art, music, scientific breakthroughs, scandals, culture, or social class issues (again, with brief introductions) in any historical period.

Learning Styles

The category of learning styles is very broad and can be broken down into preferences of instructional style, learning environment, thinking style, and expression (Purcell & Renzulli, 1998). Before deciding which of these dimensions to assess, consideration of each one and the feasibility of modifying instruction across any or all of these domains is critical.

American Literature: What is YOUR Experience?

Who is your favorite fiction writer? _____
Who is your favorite poet? _____
Who is your favorite playwright? _____
What is your favorite novel or short story? _____
What is your favorite poem? _____
What is your favorite play? _____
What fiction writer, poet, or playwright do you hope never to read
   again? _____
Which novel, poem, or play do you hope never to read again?_____
What is the first book you ever remember reading? _____
What is your favorite period of literature? _____
What is your least favorite period of literature? _____
If you had to research an author, whom would you choose to study? ___
_____
What author have you not read, but think you would like to learn more
   about? _____
What is the last book you read for pleasure? _____
What author is the most overrated and why? _____
What author is the most underrated and why?_____
What writer would you wish to emulate? _____

On the back of this page, make a list of all American literary works written before 1865 that you have read. Include novels, dramas, short stories, poems, and biographies.

Figure 4. A sample student interest and readiness survey

Note. Adapted with permission from the unpublished work of James Nutter

Instructional style preferences can be assessed by the Learning
Styles Inventory (Renzulli & Smith, 1998; Renzulli, Smith, &
Rizza, 2002), which yields data on the ways in which students
prefer to learn (e.g., lecture, peer tutoring, discussion, independent study, simulation). Instruments for assessing learning
environment preference include questions relating to both
intra- and interpersonal domains and physical preferences (e.g.,
sound, heat, light, time of day). Thinking style preferences
reflect analytical reasoning, synthetic reasoning, creative thinking, and practical and contextual reasoning (Sternberg, 1990).
Finally, expression style preferences include written, oral,

manipulative, display, dramatization, or graphic presentations of material.

Organizing and Using Preassessment Data

Examples of data that might be collected for preassessment purposes are given in Figure 5. General data is often readily available in student records, while other more specific data may need to be collected for particular units or topics of instruction. Figure 6 provides a graphic that illustrates the way in which preassessment data collected from identification materials, student cumulative files, standardized interest inventories, learning styles inventories, and teacher observation might be organized for quick referral. Teachers can use such data as a beginning point in planning units. For any given unit, the profile of individual students may be clear or the gaps in the profile may suggest that further specific achievement and readiness data or another interest assessment is warranted.

Using Figure 6, if a unit focuses on mastery of grade level mathematics concepts, a pretest can determine which objectives Tonya, Stephen, and Eric have mastered so that plans for higher level curriculum for these students can be developed. When planning for learning tasks within a unit, tasks should range from the analytic to the creative to the practical to give all students the opportunity to bring their styles of learning to the forefront and capitalize on the learning process. For further information on curriculum compacting, which provides for such steps, see Starko (1986), Reis and Renzulli (2005), and Reis, Burns, and Renzulli (1992).

Student	Exceptional Aptitude	Exceptional Achievement	Interests	Learning Style or Performance Preferences
Tonya	Very high mathematics aptitude (both on IQ subscores and PSAT taken in 7th grade); high verbal aptitude	99th percentile in math and science subtests; 90th or above in all other subtests; straight A's in math and science; grades of A's and B+ in science, social studies, language arts, and reading; teacher rates very high on learning, creativity, and reading; problem orientation	Loves math problem-solving activities; Interested in animals, has many pets; scored very high on mathematics, fine arts, and crafts on Interest-A-Lyzer	Likes to work alone; does not like to present publicly; scored low on lecture, peer tutoring; high on discussion, independent study on Learning Style Inventory (LSI); very much a practical problem orientation
Catherine	Very high verbal aptitude; average mathematics aptitude	98th percentile in reading and language arts, 95th in social studies; straight A's in reading, language arts, and social studies; grades of A's and B+ in math and science; teacher rates very high on learning, creativity, and motivation.	Has a poetry journal; scored high on creative writing, journalism, and film/video on Interest-A-Lyzer	Loves to read and write, but also likes graphic representations; very dramatic; loves working in groups; scored low on lecture; high on peer tutoring, discussion and simulation on LSI; analytic, practical, and creative synthesizer
Carol	Very high verbal aptitude; average mathematics aptitude	98th percentile in reading and language arts, 97th in social studies; straight A's in reading, language arts, and social studies; high scores in science and social studies on standardized achievement tests; teacher rates very high on learning, creativity, and motivation.	Wrote plays for her friends to perform; scored high on creative writing, journalism, and social action on Interest-A-Lyzer	Loves working in groups and loves to present; often seen discussing issues; scored low on lecture; high on peer tutoring, discussion, and simulation on LSI; analytic, practical, and creative synthesizer
Thomas	Very high verbal aptitude	95th percentile in reading and language arts; extremely high grades in introduction to Spanish in exploratory class; very high scores in science and social studies on standardized achievement tests; teacher rates very high on learning and creativity.	Loves learning about the religions of other countries; always talking about local history, topics and reporting to me about newspaper articles on local history; scored high on history and social action on Interest-A-Lyzer	Learns best by doing, not by listening or reading; scored low on lecture, peer tutoring; high on discussion, independent study on LSI; very much a practical problem orientation
Stephen	Extremely high scores on both verbal and nonverbal aptitude tests	99th percentile on all achievement subtests; straight A student; teacher rates very high on learning, creativity, and motivation.	Interested in law and legal issues, ethics and moral questions fascinate him; scored high on history and social action on Interest-A-Lyzer	Loves to read, to debate, or engage in discussion; loves simulations; great with details; scored high on lecture and discussion on LSI; very analytic thinker
Eric	Extremely high mathematics aptitude; very high in other aptitudes	99th percentile on all achievement subtests except science (80th percentile); teacher rates very high on learning and creativity; only average in motivation	Enjoys music; scored high on mathematics, business/management, and athletics on Interest-A-Lyzer	Likes to do projects at home; resists school projects; very visual; quiet, reflective, deep thinker; scored high on independent study on LSI; high on creative and analytic intelligences

Figure 5. A summary of preassessment and formative assessment tools

Data-Based Decision Making: Data Collection: Preassessment

	Standardized/Formal	Teacher Constructed Formal	Teacher Constructed Informal	Other
Aptitude	• Intelligence tests (may have verbal, nonverbal, spatial, quantitative subscores) • Specific aptitude tests • Teacher rating scales such as SRBCSS	Locally constructed teacher rating scales		
Achievement	• Standardized achievement tests (general or specific) • Standardized achievement test batteries • Teacher rating scales such as SRBCSS	Teacher rating scales pre-assessments (textbook or teacher constructed)	Teacher observations and student self-assessments	Grades in prior year or grading period
Interests	Standardized interest inventories	Interest inventories	Interviews; teacher observations	
Learning Styles/Performance Preferences Standardized/Formal	Standardized learning inventories	Teacher inventories	Student self-report; teacher observation	

Data-Based Decision Making: Data Collection: Formative Evaluation (All informal)

	Standardized/Formal	Teacher Constructed Formal	Teacher Constructed Informal	Other
Achievement	Teacher observation	Brief performance tasks; cognitive maps; homework	Student self-report	
Interests	Teacher observation		Student self-report	
Learning Styles/Performance Preferences	Teacher observation		Student self-report	

Figure 6. A summary of preassessment and formative assessment instruments

On-going

Data Collection: Formative Assessment

Whenever we begin a journey, we begin by selecting a route we believe will get us to our destination. Similarly, pre-assessment data can help pinpoint the correct first steps in engaging learners in profitable learning experiences. But, a misjudgment of the map, a malfunction in our car, a wrong turn, or a detour may create a situation where we are no longer able to make progress toward the destination. Likewise, in a learning experience or task, students may be unable to proceed as expected. As mentioned earlier, the most effective class-rooms are those where the teacher collects data during the instructional process to assess whether students are progressing effectively (Black, Harrison, Lee, Marshall, & Wiliam, 2004; Black & Wiliam, 1998). This process of formative assessment must be systematic and planned to be effective. It is *not* the old practice of giving pop quizzes or playing a "gotcha" game with students to prove they did not do assigned reading or home-work. Rather, it is a way of collecting information to allow for in-process adjustments in what is taught and to structure or modify lessons or activities to help students get back on track to achieving the goals of the lesson or unit.

Brief and Informal Formative Assessments

Even informal and brief formative assessments must reflect reliable and valid information. Quick, informal responses can be gathered simultaneously with the ongoing instructional process. For example, to assess the degree to which students are following the development of an idea, argument, process, or concept in a classroom discussion, a teacher may ask students to hold up a card indicating the degree to which they are "getting it." Students are provided *Yes, No,* or *Maybe* cards that they hold up in response; or cards might be colored green ("I am following right along."), yellow ("Caution, I may be getting lost."), or red ("Hold it! Stop! I am lost!"). The cards should be colored on only one side, so when held up, only the teacher can see the color. If students are working independently or in small groups, they might be given chips of those same colors to put on their desks, or they might be provided colored pencils to color a small dot on their paper to reflect their status. Groups working on a task together might be provided "group chips" to represent the progress of the group in achieving their goal or finishing the task. If students are working in literature circles, they can create a set of cards with a code that only the teacher knows. Such cards can be stored in pouches hanging on the back of students' chairs.

Teachers can also have students complete quick evaluations that will assist in determining each student's perception regarding the difficulty of a particular task (e.g., homework). Students take cards identifying the task's difficulty as "a breeze," "a bit of a challenge," "challenging," or "overwhelming," write their names on them, and place them into a container. Exit cards, where students turn in response slips at the end of the class or lesson, can also be valuable indicators of students' perceptions of their understanding of the day's objectives. Collection and review of homework is, of course, another means of formative assessment. Homework presents a grading issue for teachers; however, if the main goal is for students to practice or learn, then homework should not be graded. Rather, a system for recognizing attempts to complete the work and for providing feedback for improvement is more appropriate.

More Formal and More In-Depth Formative Assessment

Having students complete journal entries at the end of a class session might provide more comprehensive data. Questions such as "What were the most significant things you learned today?" will give insight into content mastery and understanding. Others like "Describe the way you went about completing the task for today. What did you do first?", "What was the most effective strategy you used today?" and "What problems did you encounter along the way?" will provide data on the student's ability to apply processes and give students practice in metacognition. Also, prompts such as "Describe what you will do next to move you closer to completing this project. What help do you need? What materials do you still need?" will provide information on the progress toward completion of projects. In a science classroom, establishing the parameters of a science journal like those used by scientists and having students keep such a journal as they explore a topic— recording how their understanding of the concepts have changed, results of their own experimentation, possible interpretations of the data, etc.—will provide useful information on how students' knowledge and understanding, as well as sophistication in processing of information, are developing.

Another way to collect data is to give students a mini-task to complete when they have achieved the instructional goal that parallels some aspect of the performance expected. For example, returning to the unit on colonization, ask them to choose a colony and write a brief letter back to their families in the "old country" describing, from their point of view, what their purpose was in coming to the New World, what they encountered in this new situation, and how things are progressing. Ask them to provide historical evidence that supports their conclusions. Using a rubric to assess their progress will afford data to adjust instruction, and sharing this information will provide feedback to the students on areas of strength and weakness.

Related to both the journal entries and the mini–tasks is the establishment of portfolios, where teachers and students can work collaboratively in the formative evaluation process and build a product that can also be used for summative purposes. The added benefit of the portfolio is that it provides a basis for students' self-assessment and offers the opportunity to reflect on learning. Johnson and Rose (1997) stress that a portfolio is *not* a collection of student work arbitrarily thrown together, nor is it just a writing folder into which students' compositions are collected, nor is it a collection of student tests. A portfolio is a "purposeful, systematic anthology of a student's work over time that includes student participation in the collection of content, evidence of student self-reflection, criteria for selection, criteria for judging merit" (Johnson & Rose, p. 6).

The selection of entries into a portfolio should be a collaborative effort between the student and teacher with a clear explanation of reasons why products have been selected for inclusion. Entries should demonstrate that goals of instruction have been achieved and reflect growth and progress toward learning goals. Johnson and Rose provide descriptions of ways in which products such as writing samples (including multiple drafts of published pieces, letters, essays, reports, and creative writing), conceptual maps, sketches, artwork, photographs, audiotapes, videotapes, school awards, and tests can be used for assessment through portfolios. They also offer guidance for selecting items for portfolios and provide checklists, surveys, and rating scales that may be useful to teachers and students for evaluating portfolio entries. One such checklist is provided in Figure 7.

Self-Evaluation for Reviewing Portfolios

Name: _____Date: _____

When you can check "yes" for each item and have written down your list of artifacts, you are ready to have your teacher conference.

Have I included an introduction to my portfolio?   Yes   No

Does my introduction explain what is in my portfolio?   Yes   No

The artifacts I chose to place in my portfolio were:

Do the artifacts I chose show my learning growth?   Yes   No

Have I explained how I chose each artifact?   Yes   No

Have I included self-evaluation that shows my strengths?   Yes   No

Have I included self-evaluations that show my areas that
need improvements?   Yes   No

Have I included my goals to improve my learning?   Yes   No

Are my goals ones I can reach and that challenge me?   Yes   No

Have I included a way to respond to my portfolio?   Yes   No

Figure 7. Student Checklist for reviewing portfolios

Note. From *Portfolios: Clarifying, Constructing, and Enhancing* (p. 252), by N. J. Johnson and L. M. Rose, 1997, Lancaster, PA: Technomic. Copyright ©1997 by Rowman & Littlefield Education. Reprinted with permission.

Formative Self-Assessment Data

Teachers can also help students collect data for self-assessment. Regularly presenting two multiple-choice or open-ended response questions at the beginning or end of a class, and then providing time for a quick review of answers and any clarification questions will give students a sense of how well they are grasping concepts and learning new skills. These items may be differentiated according to the level of expectations as the lessons have been tiered or adjusted for difficulty, complexity, or level of sophistication. Posting a series of questions on the board and asking students to attempt the two that are easiest for them and two they perceive to be the most difficult will give students the opportunity to see what they have learned and where challenges exist.

Use of Tests to Assess Learner Outcomes

Traditionally, paper-and-pencil tests have dominated class-room assessment in upper elementary, middle school, and high school. Most of these tests are some combination of true/false, multiple-choice, matching, fill-in-the-blank, and short and extended essay questions. There are many advantages of using multiple-choice or other objective formats in assessment: (1) the range of knowledge, understandings, and skills that can be assessed in a relatively short period of time is very broad, (2) the instruments can be administered to large groups and scored quickly, and (3) they generally are very reliable. The disadvantage of such assessments, particularly in measuring many of the goals and objectives of gifted programs, are the limited range of outcomes measured, and the potential for a mismatch between the high-level goals and objectives that should be set for gifted students, and those typically measured by such tests. Further, objective-based items can only measure fragmented bits of knowledge and understanding. While there are some examples of objective tests and multiple-choice test items that do measure complex thinking, the construction of such items requires considerable care and very careful attention to ensure the student is, in fact, required to use higher level thinking, rather than simply memory, to respond correctly.

Performance and Product Assessments

Many of the goals and objectives that appropriately represent elevated expectations for gifted students cannot be assessed by traditional paper-and-pencil tests. Any goals that suggest the integration of sophisticated, complex, and in-depth understanding; creative productivity; the investigation of authentic problems; the use of alternative means of expression; or performance that emulates or represents that of professionals must be assessed using performance and product assessments. These products or performances may be elicited by very specific task descriptions or prompts that require reflection of increased depth, complexity, abstractness, and/or sophisticated understanding of state or local curricular standards. Or, they may be used to assess specific goals that are derived from enrichment of the traditional curricula. These assessments may also include open-ended tasks and product expectations that reflect outcomes of independent study or in-depth investigation of problems or issues selected by students. In either case, they should allow for all students to engage in the demonstration of their learning and achievement based on clear standards that represent appropriate expectations for gifted students and ways of dealing with advanced content, sophisticated process, and authentic products.

Figure 8 provides an example of a structured prompt where a gifted student's curriculum has been modified and is now being assessed. This particular assessment allows the students to use both written and oral presentations to demonstrate achievement of the goals. In this particular case, the students are limited to these modes of expression due to the integration of specific language arts objectives relating to

An Analysis of Oppression

You are an advisor to the Secretary of State. As advisor, you are part of a network of experts who help the U.S. government maintain peaceful and effective

communication with other countries. The job entails working with the Secretary of State to strategize important political negotiations and discussions with the world's most powerful leaders. Your studies in political science have led others to view you as a valuable commodity because of your specialization in the psychological and sociological perspectives/theories of war.

You have learned through the years that understanding the motives and behaviors of governments and individuals in history helps us to avoid repeating atrocious mistakes. As you know from your studies, throughout history, stories of war have been dominated by acts of oppression. It has happened over and over again, in every war, in every time period. In your meetings with the Secretary of State, you often reference specific events of past wars and compare/contrast those events with current events. In particular, you concentrate on similarities and differences in governments' and peoples' responses to oppression.

Recently, you have been observing the events in the current world conflict with growing concern. There appear to be many parallels between the situation in the current world conflict and the events leading to Hitler's rise in Nazi Germany. Based on what you know about people and governments' responses to oppression, you fear that some of the same horrors of Nazi Germany may repeat themselves in the current conflict. You have been asked to present your concerns and recommendations to the President, the Secretary of State, and a committee of political advisors in both a 10-minute oral presentation and an accompanying paper. The breakdown and outline of your task follows.

Part One
*   Review the events of Hitler's rise in Nazi Germany. How did the Holocaust begin? Why do you think things happened as they did and when they did? How did the Jewish people react to Hitler's brand of prejudice and oppression? How did the outside world react?
*   Consult several sources about oppression in general. Why does it happen? How do groups react to being oppressed? To being the oppressors?
*   Prepare a social psychological analysis of reasons why the German people felt it was right to treat the Jewish people as they did and why the Jewish people reacted to their horrible treatment as they did.

Figure 8. A sample performance task

Part Two
- Using your analysis in Part One, compare and contrast the events leading to oppression in Nazi Germany and the escalation of the current conflict. You may wish to include references to theories about aggression, power, and prejudice.
- What did you learn about oppression in Nazi Germany that you can apply to current events? How are the motives/reactions of the people/governments similar? How are they different? How do they relate to time and place? Given what you know about the outcome of oppression in Nazi Germany, what can you predict about the outcome of current world conflict?
- Apply the same analysis you used in Part One to the problems in the current world conflict and use examples from Nazi Germany to make an argument for the validity of your analysis and for your predictions about the current situation.

Part Three
- Take a position on the actions occurring in the chosen current world situation. What do you think our government should do to prevent some of the heinous crimes of history? Urge the President to proceed as you advise, based on your analysis of past events, as well as your understanding of current events. Be sure to outline the predicted results of heeding your advice, as well as the likely consequences of not following your recommendations.

The presentation should cover all three parts outlined above. All parts should flow together. The presentation of your research in Parts One and Two should logically support and lead into your presentation of Part Three. The entire presentation may not exceed 10 minutes. Include visuals and/or supporting resources to help clearly convey your ideas.

The paper should cover all three parts of the task in an elegant and coherent manner, using sophisticated vocabulary, strong imagery, and clear prose. It should serve as an extension of your presentation. Anyone looking for more information about the points you cover in the presentation should be able to consult the paper for elaboration on your topic.

Please include a bibliography of the sources used in both the presentation and paper.

Evaluation of the task is based on the accuracy of mentioned events from Nazi Germany and the current world conflict, the thoroughness of your analysis of oppression and its various components, the applications and generalizations made from that analysis, and the recommendations given to the President, the Secretary of State, and other advisors for action in the current conflict. In addition, the style, delivery, and mechanics of your paper and presentation are part of the evaluation criteria. See rubrics for specific criteria and performance descriptions.

Figure 8. A sample performance task, continued

writing and oral presentation that were incorporated into the unit objectives. If that were not the case, then the teacher could plan for more open-ended presentation modes; however, in all cases the task should be clearly evaluated according to criteria for both form and substance. Additional examples of tasks, rubrics, and other assessment tools can be found in Callahan (2005).

Other products or performances to be evaluated may result from long-term assignments or projects that meet the requirements of models such as the Schoolwide Enrichment Model (Renzulli & Reis, 1985), which requires students to devise solutions to real problems and present them to authentic audiences. The Schoolwide Enrichment Model includes Type I exploratory activities designed to expose students to a wide variety of disciplines not ordinarily studied in school with the goal of stimulating new interests in students. Type II activities in the model are designed as process or skill-building activities in the cognitive domain. In these activities students might learn how to use critical thinking skills; they might be involved in projects to develop their creative thinking or to develop skills in written, oral, or visual communication. The Type I and Type II activities are both designed to help create ideas for, and to solidify interests in, involvement in Type III enrichment, which focuses on individual and small group investigations of real problems. An example of one item on a rating scale used to evaluate products produced by students completing a Type III activity is provided in Figure 9.

It is not sufficient to create the task and leave the definition of expectations and standards to chance or to comparative evaluation. It is critical that standards and rubrics used to evaluate student products reflect the highest level of performance (Wiggins, 1996). Once appropriate standards of excellence or expert performance have been identified, educators must ensure that the rubrics used to evaluate the student clearly describe the progression of development from novice level to expert performance. Schack (1994) has effectively outlined

Selection of appropriate reference materials, resource person, equipment	
Novice	Uses only secondary source materials such as encyclopedias and textbooks; no original sources or original data; reads like a "report" that was synthesized from other's thinking
Apprentice	Uses some original sources but only with limited applicability to the problem selected; fails to see the problem as one where the tools of a profession are applied
Emerging	Incorporates primary source data, original experimental outcome data, or other data that leads to a creative production solution or the production of an original product, but there are a few errors in interpretation or fails to carefully evaluate the data
Master	Accurately incorporates primary source data, original experimental outcome data, or other data that leads to a creative production solution or the production of an original product; uses the "tools" of the profession in terms of references, data collection strategies, resource people, and/or equipment

Figure 9. Sample criterion and levels for a Type III Project

such a rubric for adolescent research projects. The dimensions along which she suggests evaluating research projects include:

- formulating the research question,
- generating hypotheses,
- determining sample selections,
- selecting and implementing data gathering techniques,
- representing and analyzing data,
- drawing conclusions, and
- reporting findings.

Wiggins (1996) has provided general dimensions along which the work of gifted students should be scored. The first important criterion he identifies is *impact*. Within this general category, he provides guiding questions for evaluating the degree of effectiveness, the level of quality, and the process of creating the product:

- Does the product created solve the problem?
- Does it persuade an audience? (Degree of effectiveness)
- Is the product outstanding in its class? Is it novel? Is it ethical? (Level of quality)
- Is the process of creation purposeful?
- Was the process efficient? Was it adaptive? Was the creator self-critical? (Process)
- Was the process of creation thoughtful (considerate, responsive, inquisitive, etc.)?
- Does the student use the appropriate skills? These skills would be those linked to the task and endeavor and would be situation-specific for each product.

Wiggins also recommends that the *form* of the product be rated. Is it well-designed? Does form follow function? Is it authentic? Is it elegant? Is it clever? To determine whether a product is well-crafted, he provides guidelines for considering organization, the preciseness, clarity, and mechanical soundness, among others. *Style* is the third dimension Wiggins identifies as important in rating gifted student products. He recommends consideration of an authentic voice and gracefulness (as might be exhibited in a performance, i.e., a dance). And, as expected, Wiggins considers the *content* to be important. He includes accuracy (e.g., correctness, validity), sophistication (e.g., depth, insightfulness, power, expertise), and aptness (focus) within this category.

Wiggins also provides examples of ways in which exemplary models have been collected that set the highest level of performance required for gifted students. Looking at the work of older students and examining the models of experts can help students articulate ascending levels of expertise. Students might also identify accomplished works and develop criteria for

achieving high levels of performance from their own understanding of excellence. Other ideas for creating tasks for gifted
students and generic rubrics for performance-based assessments are outlined by Lewin and Shoemaker (1998); Marzano,
Pickering, and McTighe (1993); and Karnes and Stephens
(1999).

Specific outcomes should be reflected in the tasks developed by the teacher and the rubrics used to assess them. A section of a rubric designed to evaluate the task illustrated
previously in Figure 8 and structured to address the range of
performance of highly able learners is presented in Figure 10.

While these scales were designed for teacher assessment of
student progress, students should be encouraged to use these
scales to evaluate their own work and that of their peers. Such
self-evaluation skills provide a base for students to develop
intrinsic standards of performance. Using the scales to evaluate
others also can be valuable in helping students understand academic standards, by allowing them to see models of each level
and discuss the meaning of the levels of performance.

Certainly the observation of musical and artistic performance will use carefully developed performance assessment
rubrics. However, as mentioned earlier, teachers may do more
informal assessments of student behaviors relevant to the goals
of instruction. In particular, outcomes that are in the affective
realm are often assessed using more informal observational
strategies. Often checklists or rating scales are used to accom-
plish this assessment in a systematic fashion. An example of a
rubric used to evaluate working attitudes and behaviors is provided in Figure 11.

While many process dimensions have been included in the
assessments described above as summative evaluations, process
skills may be assessed independently as part of either formative
or summative evaluation. The evaluation of work habits, the
ability to contribute to group productivity, and the development of higher level thinking and questioning skills may be part
of a rubric or may be assessed through teacher observation of

Analytical Scoring Rubric	Master Advisor	Experienced Advisor	Novice Advisor
Authenticity	Examples and references to historical and current events are accurate. You bring the complexity of the Holocaust and of the current situation to your audience in an understandable and accurate way. Facts are carefully checked and include the most significant details.	Examples and references to historical and current events are accurate with the exception of one or two minor facts. Still, the audience gets a feel for what happened during the Holocaust and what is happening in the current conflict.	Examples and references to historical and current events have too many gaps in accuracy OR significant details are left out of some important Holocaust and/or current events. The audience has trouble understanding the issues involved.
Writing Style	Examples and references to historical and current events are accurate. You bring the complexity of the Holocaust and of the current situation to your audience in an understandable and accurate way. Facts are carefully checked and include the most significant details.	The paper is tailored to the audience although a few references are made to ideas that the reader wouldn't know. In some places, passive voice is used. Included are a clear introduction, body, and conclusion that center on a theme. Occasionally, the transitions are choppy.	The paper is not tailored to the audience. Too many or too few assumptions are made about what the reader knows. In some/many places, passive voice is used. It is difficult to follow a single theme throughout the paper and only a few supporting details are provided within an unclear structure.

Figure 10. A sample of scoring for the written section of the performance task Analysis of Oppression

Dimensions	Exemplary	Developed	Emerging	Undeveloped
Focus and good concentration (To what extent does the student give full attention to the work being done?)	Keenly focused and/or listening closely to whomever is speaking without adult supervision or reminders. Does not distract others.	Shows interest in the task at hand; rarely distracts others and needs minimal supervision or reminders.	Sometimes distracted or may distract others, but responds immediately to reminders by an adult.	Easily distracted and often off task; distracts others from the task at hand; does not respond positively to peer or adult reminders.
Persistence (To what extent does the student work toward continuous improvement without giving up?)	Takes charge and maintain ownership of own learning. Works toward continuous improvement and is open to any help offered, conscientiously choosing how to use that advice. Does not give up, even if the task becomes difficult at times.	Works conscientiously toward improvement and seeks help when experiencing difficulty (prior to the point of failure). Requires little encouragement to keep trying.	Works toward improvement when directed to do so, but needs encouragement. Seeks help when experiencing failure or when advised to do so. Needs a lot of encouragement and prodding to keep trying.	Demonstrates little interest in improvement; gives up easily and does not seek help when needed or when advised to do so. Does not respond to encouragement and rarely acts on given advice or help. Sometimes gives up without really trying.

Figure 11. A rubric for scoring work habits

Note. Compiled from "Students Helping Students" by C. Shepardson, 2001, *Parenting for High Potential*, p. 4, 30. Copyright ©2001 by National Association for Gifted Children. Reprinted with permission.

Student Name: _____

For each item below rate the student's behavior based on the following scale:
1. The student nearly always exhibits this behavior (> 90% of the time)
2. The student usually exhibits this behavior (more than half of the time)
3. The student sometimes exhibits this behavior (10–50% of the time)
4. The student seldom exhibits this behavior (< 10% of the time)
5. No opportunity to observe this behavior

A. Use of reasoning and thinking skills
1. Provides support for statements   1 2 3 4 5
2. Provides concise clarification and extension   1 2 3 4 5
3. Suggests possible limitations of statements   1 2 3 4 5
4. Avoids overgeneralization   1 2 3 4 5

B. Group dynamics
1. Follows focus of the discussion   1 2 3 4 5
2. Responds appropriately to others, respecting their ideas   1 2 3 4 5
3. Avoids interrupting others   1 2 3 4 5
4. Demonstrates the ability to view situations from others'
    perspectives   1 2 3 4 5
5. Builds on the ideas of others   1 2 3 4 5
6. Questions other students appropriately (asking them to
    support, clarify, or extend their ideas)   1 2 3 4 5
7. Demonstrates respect for opinions, ideas, and values of
    others   1 2 3 4 5

C. Other
1. Can accurately self-monitor behavior   1 2 3 4 5
2. Accurately self-evaluates   1 2 3 4 5

Figure 12. Group discussion skills

student behaviors in class. The rating scale in Figure 12 is an example of a teacher rating scale that might be used during discussions to assess development of students' thinking processes and growth in interactive skills.

Now that the outcomes from a unit of instruction are measured, the obvious next step is consideration of how such data will be used. Of course, reporting to parents and students on the degree to which students have achieved the goals of instruction is the primary purpose of summative data collection. If a wide range of assessment tools have been used that allow students to demonstrate their highest level of accomplishment, then all parties will have a clearer understanding of the achievements and progress of students. This data can also serve to form a new instructional cycle, as it provides information on knowledge, understanding, skills, and such affective dimensions as habits of mind, attitudes, emerging interests, and favored learning styles.

When each stage of the instructional process has been supported and enhanced by an assessment process that reliably and validly gathers data on students' aptitude, prior achievement and readiness, interests, and learning styles, student learning is also enhanced. Investment in learning about the student and responding to that knowledge with learning activities that are engaging, motivating, and within the appropriate range of difficulty is rewarded with learners who maximize the use of instructional time to produce outcomes that are reflective of the highest possible accomplishments.

References

Black, P., Harrison, C., Lee, C., Marshall, B., & Wiliam, D. (2004). Working inside the black box: Assessment for learning in the classroom. *Phi Delta Kappan, 86*, 21.

Black, P., & Wiliam, D. (1998). Inside the black box: Raising standards through classroom assessment. *Phi Delta Kappan, 80*, 139–144.

Bransford, J. D., Brown, A. L., & Cocking, R. R. (Eds.). (1999). *How people learn: Brain, mind, experience and school.* Washington, DC: National Academy Press.

Callahan, C. M. (2005). Making the grade or achieving the goal. In F. A. Karnes & S. M. Bean (Eds.), *Methods and materials for teaching the gifted* (pp. 211–244). Waco, TX: Prufrock Press.

Cobb, P. (1994, September). *Theories of mathematical learning and constructivism: A personal view.* Paper presented at the Symposium on Trends and Perspectives in Mathematics Education, Institute for Mathematics, University of Klagenfurt, Austria.

Johnson, N. J., & Rose, L. M. (1997). *Portfolios: Clarifying, constructing, and enhancing.* Lancaster, PA: Technomic.

Karnes, F. A., & Stephens, K. R. (1999). *The ultimate guide to student product development and evaluation.* Waco, TX: Prufrock Press.

Lewin, L., & Shoemaker, B. J. (1998). *Great performances: Creating classroom-based assessment tasks.* Alexandria, VA: Association for Supervision and Curriculum Development.

Marzano, R. J., Pickering, D., & McTighe, J. (1993). *Assessing student outcomes: Performance assessment using the dimensions of learning model.* Alexandria, VA: Association for Supervision and Curriculum Development.

Piaget, J. (1978). *Success and understanding.* Cambridge, MA: Harvard University Press.

Purcell, J. H., & Renzulli, J. S. (1998). *Total talent portfolio: A systematic plan to identify and nurture gifts and talents.* Mansfield Center, CT: Creative Learning Press.

Reis, S. M., Burns, D. E., & Renzulli, J. S. (1992). *Curriculum compacting: The complete guide to modifying the regular curriculum for high ability students.* Mansfield Center, CT: Creative Learning.

Reis, S. M., & Renzulli, J. S. (2005). *Curriculum compacting: An easy start to differentiating for high-potential students.* Waco, TX: Prufrock Press.

Renzulli, J. S. (1997). *Interest-a-lyzer family of instruments.* Mansfield Center, CT: Creative Learning Press.

Renzulli, J. S., & Reis, S. M. (1985). *The Schoolwide Enrichment Model: A comprehensive plan for educational excellence.* Mansfield Center, CT: Creative Learning Press.

Renzulli, J. S., & Smith, L. (1998). *The Learning Styles Inventory: A measure of student preference for instructional technique.* Mansfield Center, CT: Creative Learning Press.

Renzulli, J. S., Smith, L., & Rizza, M. G. (2002). *Learning styles inventory—Version III.* Mansfield Center, CT: Creative Learning Press.

Renzulli, J. S., Smith, L. H., White, A. J., Callahan, C. M., Hartman, R. K., & Westberg, K. L. (2004). *Scales for Rating the Behavioral Characteristics of Superior Students.* Mansfield Center, CT: Creative Learning Press.

Ryser, G. R., & Johnsen, S. K. (1998). *Test of Mathematical Abilities for Gifted Students.* Waco, TX: Prufrock Press.

Schack, G. D. (1994). Authentic assessment procedures for secondary students' original research. *Journal of Secondary Gifted Education, 6,* 38–43.

Starko, A. J. (1986). *It's about time: Inservice strategies for curriculum compacting.* Mansfield Center, CT: Creative Learning Press.

Sternberg, R. J. (1990). Thinking styles: Keys to understanding student performance. *Phi Delta Kappan, 71,* 366–371.

Vygotsky, L. S. (1978). *Mind in society: The development of higher psychological processes.* Cambridge, MA: Harvard University Press.

Wiggins, G. (1996). Anchoring assessment with exemplars: Why students and teachers need models. *Gifted Child Quarterly, 40,* 66–69.

About the Author

Carolyn M. Callahan, Commonwealth Professor and department chair at the Curry School of Education at the University of Virginia, is currently the director of the University of Virginia site of the National Research Center on the Gifted and Talented. She has written more than 160 articles and 40 book chapters on a broad range of topics in gifted education, including the areas of the identification of gifted students, the evaluation of gifted programs, the development of performance assessments, issues facing gifted females, and gifted program options. She has received the Distinguished Scholar and Service Award from the National Association of Gifted Children and the Outstanding Faculty Award from the Commonwealth of Virginia.